Ballington Booth

New York's Inferno Explored

Scenes Full of Pathos Powerfully Portrayed-Siberian Desolation Caused by

Vice and Drink Tenements Packed with Misery and Crime

Ballington Booth

New York's Inferno Explored
Scenes Full of Pathos Powerfully Portrayed-Siberian Desolation Caused by Vice and Drink Tenements Packed with Misery and Crime

ISBN/EAN: 9783337277680

Printed in Europe, USA, Canada, Australia, Japan

Cover: Foto ©Suzi / pixelio.de

More available books at **www.hansebooks.com**

NEW YORK'S

INFERNO

EXPLORED.

───◆───

SCENES FULL OF PATHOS POWERFULLY PORTRAYED
—SIBERIAN DESOLATION CAUSED BY VICE
AND DRINK—TENEMENTS PACKED
WITH MISERY AND CRIME.

───◆───

BY

COMMISSIONER & MRS. BALLINGTON BOOTH.

───◆───

NEW YORK:
PRINTED AND PUBLISHED AT THE SALVATION ARMY HEADQUARTERS,
111 READE STREET.
───
1891.

CONTENTS TABLE.

The Salvation Army.

NATIONAL HEADQUARTERS: 111 READE STREET, NEW YORK CITY.

———•◆•———

April 15th, 1891.

It could be readily understood were we pleading for the life
of one condemned to die, or for the
pardon of one on whom judgment had
already been passed, that we should

experience difficulty in finding
language to express the feelings
which would weigh upon our hearts.
We are not at the bar pleading for
the life of one or two, but we
strive to plead with the conscience
--the human sympathy--the brother-
feeling--of the happy and fortunate
on behalf of the many despairing
ones, hidden from them by the night
darkness in which they live.

It is no easy task, with the
full and only too real memory of the
depths of blight and ruin by which
we have just been surrounded, to even
faintly picture to others what our
minds and hearts still vividly see,

Every form of vice and iniquity that can be admitted in the gap between theism and atheism, between heaven and hell, exists in the underworld of death with which we have just been brought face to face.

With the knowledge of this we have returned to prosecute with intenser zeal and deeper love the work of lifting the fallen and saving the lost.

It must be action, not sentiment; deeds, not words.

Shelter must be found for the weary head of the homeless tramp. More saviours must be raised up for the rescue of abandoned and hopeless women, who dwell in this shadow of death.   Salvation must be proclaimed in love in the ears of those now filled only with curses and blasphemy.

These pages will fall into the hands of many who will never hear our voices--who, though unknown to us, are known to our God by the beatings of heart in sympathy with humanity. To these we appeal. Help us, that we may better help these helpless, loveless ones; and of them it may also be said, " I was an hungered, and ye gave me meat: I was thirsty, and ye gave me drink: I was a stranger, and ye took me in:

naked, and ye clothed me: I was
sick and ye visited me."

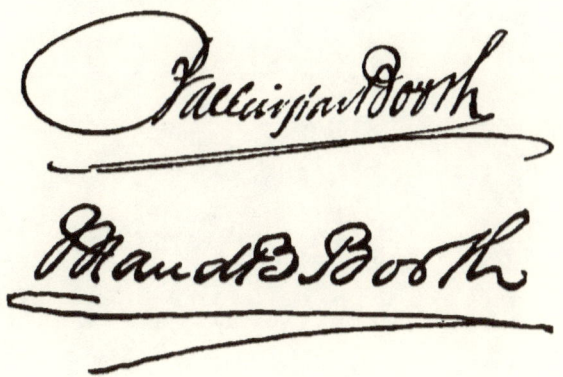

NEW YORK'S INFERNO.

MR. BOOTH IN THE SLUMS.

WANTED—A RIVER OF SOCIAL PURITY TO CLEANSE THE LABYRINTH OF NEW YORK CITY.

E have read how Hercules, the mythical hero, cleansed in one day the stables of Augeas, King of Elis, in which 3,000 oxen had stood for thirty years, by changing the course of and leading through them the two rivers, Alpheus and Peneus. But such a vision of human depravity and hard suffering as the one I have just witnessed in the heart of this great city causes me to yearn that it were possible for a river of Divine power and social purity to sweep over it, that the waters thereof might cleanse it from its festering evil and cankering vice.

11

With faith in the Latin proverb that " The true knowledge of things must be derived from the things themselves," I was disposed to withhold any very pronounced opinions of the baser side of New York city until I had myself had the opportunity of visiting some of its denser and darker neighborhoods.

In accordance with a long desired undertaking, I with two companions—an officer and soldier in the Salvation Army—resolved to disguise myself, and in a rough and ragged garb, which I was assured presented a most unkempt and shaggy appearance, and which wou'd admit of my passing unsuspected even among more dangerous members of a Bowery "gang," I spent some time as one among the crowd of darkest America.

I had somewhat prepared myself for revelations of moral decay and vicious life in this social quagmire. I had heard again and again what one and another had said of this plague spot of sin and death and I had seen many of its denizens.

But all previous accounts and descriptions became obliterated from my memory by the surprise and horror I experienced when passing through some of the foul haunts and vicious hotbeds which make up the labyrinth of this modern Sodom—I had almost said the Inferno of America's greatest city.

CHAPTER I.

SORROW BY THE WAYSIDE.

IT was nine o'clock p. m. when I turned into our headquarters on Reade street to change my dress and don my ill-fitting and tattered clothes. The whirl and activity of that precinct of the great city had now been hushed, and a mantle of silence was thrown over the buildings which a few hours before had worn all the appearance of life and bustle.

Leaving my watch and papers with a staff officer I sallied forth with my two companions up the dark streets in the direction of the Bowery. The wind, by no means strong, was nevertheless piercing and chilling. The darkness was thick, and helped to make more glaring the electric lights. Here and there a policeman eyed us curiously, if not suspiciously from beneath the brim of his helmet. On, on we tramped toward the quarters where the darkness of each night hides from the eyes of the pure and good ten thousand sins which lengthen the black catalogue of hell.

I had not to wait to reach the Bowery to see a sight which would cause every pure father a shudder of horror and bring to the cheek of every true mother a blush of shame. The doors of a low saloon at a street corner opened suddenly and two men stepped upon the sidewalk holding up a young woman by her arms. Young did I say? She was not only young, but fair and beautiful in face, yet awful to relate, was so drunk that it was with difficulty that they could prevent her from falling on the sidewalk.

" It is all right," said one of the men, looking across to the

13

other with a wink, and with a grin upon his countenance he
signed to his companion to turn up a certain street, and they
disappeared into the darkness.

We shortly reached the Bowery and had turned from its
many lighted and thronged sidewalks and were making for

COMMISSIONER BOOTH IN SLUM COSTUME.

Water street when we beheld two half clad little girls come
out of a dingy, low-looking saloon. Their tiny faces looked
blue with cold and pinched with hunger. As I stopped for a
few seconds I overheard the older say, "No use waiting any

longer, he won't come," then I thought of my little three-year-old boy safe at home in his cot, and of the thousands of children who at that hour would be tucked snugly in their beds protected from the crushing blight and degradation which would fall upon the lives of the little hungry ones who were running past us with bare heads and naked feet.

AMONG HORRORS.

We turned into Water street—a street of death. It was difficult to believe, as we glanced first to the right and then to the left, that we were in a Christian country. Painted, dressed in bright colors, sitting in the windows and at the doors, were shameless women calling upon those who were passing to enter, and as the horror of the surroundings unfolded itself in my mind the words of the sage rang in my ears :—" Her mouth is smoother than oil, but her end is bitter as wormwood, sharp as a two edged sword. Her feet go down to death, her steps take hold on hell."

Here and there on this "dark and black night" a man could be seen to enter one of these places (aye and lads appearing less than sixteen) " as an ox goeth to the slaughter."

While passing along only one block we counted no less than forty-eight prostitutes sitting in the doorways and windows of this street of death. Nor is this quarter (incredible as the number of women who were soliciting may seem) the worst rendezvous or resort for fallen women in this precinct.

Another street—the name of which, for the sake of the visits our Slum Brigade are successfully making there, I withhold—presented an even more horrible sight. Standing at the corner of the block and looking down the street I was dumbfounded—almost paralyzed. The incessant low shuffling of feet, reminding one of the tread of fallen spirits, was all one could hear, save the low whisperings and murmurings of the women as one and another of the opposite sex passed them.

Oh, it was awful! As I stood there within sound of the footsteps of despairing women I was reminded that one gentleman engaged in this work had recently estimated that there are from fifteen to twenty thousand prostitutes in the cities of New York and Brooklyn. I could scarcely believe that such a condition of affairs as I then witnessed existed in this city, where so many Christians have of late soothed themselves and congratulated their countrymen upon the need in "Darkest England" being so much greater than in Darkest America.

A TOUCHING ENCOUNTER.

We counted along this street, in the length of only one block, thirty-eight women waiting about. I have rarely ever experienced such gratitude as while looking upon these poor, down-trodden creatures for the nightly mission and vigilance of the Slum Brigade, two of whom we shortly afterward quite unexpectedly saw when passing along Cherry street.

It was a scene that could not fail to impress any man though he carried a heart of stone. We were standing upon the threshold of a large saloon. The strains of music and wild mirth fell strangely upon our ears. At a table opposite the bar sat a young woman with her head bent. In front of her were glasses containing newly-drawn liquor, but her thoughts were not dwelling upon the contents of the glass before her, and even the music seemed to lose its charm; her mind was being carried back to vows made beneath some kind parental roof, and her heart was for a few moments directed to the goodness and mercy of One who nearly nineteen hundred years ago allowed His feet to be washed with the tears and wiped with the hair of a fallen woman.

Around her shoulders was the loving arm of a slum sister,

who was speaking in terms of gentleness and mercy to her of a nobler, higher and truer life which she might live. What a look of conviction is stamped upon her countenance as that slum savior, on behalf of the Saviour of Nazareth, deals faithfully with the girl in the midst of those surroundings of dancing, revelry and sin!

We pushed the door a little further open, and as a woman rushed to bid us enter the other slum sister looked up—it was *my wife!*

But a few seconds at that door was all the time we could spare and our feet must hasten on to other and yet darker centres of the great city.

While making our way past coarse looking men and hopeless looking women, memory recalled the efforts of these Saviour-like slum workers to me. But an hour before I had entered their quarters and shaken hands with them. They were sparsely furnished, there being only plain wooden chairs and tables, only a small-sized stove and no carpet ; but it was scrupulously clean, and I could understand how the warmth and brightness, to say nothing of the cheerful and saved faces of those in this slum home, would be brightening to those who had to walk about through the cheerless night without.

I recalled the bitter incident which the officer in charge had related to me of the miserable room where she had found amid extreme squalor and filth, a babe dying. The parents were drunkards—there were two other little children. A few minutes after she entered the frail infant breathed its last in her arms.

They then washed the infant and prepared to lay it out for burial, but they had no place on which to lay the dead child, and had to use the sides of an old packing case for this purpose. The next morning, upon calling at this miserable abode, they found both father and mother drunk—drunk, with their dead infant lying a few feet from them !

It is in such abodes as these, I recollected, that a ray of comfort, truth and salvation is taken by these slum workers ; and as I drew my tattered coat closer around me and passed along in the glare of the saloons, I raised my heart from that benighted centre in gratitude to God for this branch of Salvation Army work.

CHAPTER II.

IN THE CHEAP LODGING HOUSES.

FOR some time it had been brought forcibly home to us that there were many men in this great city homeless and shelterless who seldom take off their coats and boots, and for whom there are few lodging houses where they can get clean and efficient accommodation and quiet repose. Not, however, until we saw with our own eyes the miserable and tired features of scores of men walking through the long, bitter nights, cold and hungry, could we credit the inefficiency and discomfort of the lodging houses for out-of-work and homeless men.

Resolved upon gaining some personal experience of one of these lodging houses, in company with one of my companions I presented myself at the small narrow pigeonhole, through which we made our united request for " a place to sleep." A head was at once lowered and the two eyes scrutinized closely and suspiciously my long form and then the shorter one of my companion. Their owner having satisfied himself that the two applicants were sufficiently rough on the exterior to be allowed to pass on the payment of ten cents apiece, opened a door and we stepped over the threshold. But what a sight confronted us !

I drew back almost bewildered, wondering whether my eyes had not for once utterly deceived me. Could it be possible that into a room about 20 by 25 feet, filled with the smoke of tobacco and the strong fumes of drink, so musty and close that one almost staggered under the atmosphere,

BACK TO BACK.—SIXTY-FIVE MEN IN ONE ROOM.

some sixty-five to seventy men lay back to back huddled together on the floor like swine? Some were fully dressed, others partially, others again were almost destitute of clothing.

For a few moments I and my companion stood as if riveted to the floor.

The man having charge of the room had risen from a low stool, with a greasy wooden pipe in his mouth, from which the smoke of bad tobacco coiled up just under our faces, and opening a side door he beckoned us to follow him. We did so, but slowly, lest we should step upon some of the bodies that crowded the floor. Ten cents each we had paid, and for this we were to be favored with better accommodation than those crowding the boards at five cents per head.

"That is your bunk." said the manager, slapping the miserable covering of the narrow crib, which I at a glance discovered lay in rather too close proximity to the one as uninviting beneath it.

"And that is yours," he said, turning to my companion, pointing to another as he twisted his pipe into the opposite side of a mouth denoting sternness and greed. Then the door was closed, and we were left standing amid the slumbering and slumberless inmates of that lodging house.

ALL ONE TO THE GOVERNOR.

"What shall we do?" I whispered over to my companion and at the same instant took a hurried survey of the sleepers. Hard faces, worn features and sad expressions bespoke the weary and too oft fruitless hunt for work and the cruel struggle to keep off the gaunt wolf of hunger, which struggle slowly but too surely kills the victim or drives him to *despair*.

Sleep! Talk of sleeping in the poisoned, loathsome atmosphere of that room! I have read of the impure and fetid

A FIVE-CENT LODGING HOUSE.

air which filled the pestilential prisons of those incarcerated during the long struggle in the South, but it would be difficult to imagine it worse than that which I breathed in that stifling lodging house.

Having satisfied myself that the surroundings were such as few even of the lowest type of humanity could endure, I turned to my companion saying, "Let us go."

"Governor," I said in an undertone, "are you always as full as this?"

"I guess pretty nearly always," was the reply.

"Well, I say, governor, I think this is too full for us, and that we'll go elsewhere," I remarked.

"Say, boss," chimed in my companion, "I can't stand this."

"I don't care. I've got your twenty cents," was the gruff and quick reply.

We turned away from the door into the piercing, chilling wind, which, though such a contrast, was preferable to the thick, choking atmosphere within, to wonder how the poor, penniless tramp must feel who has fallen low in the social scale and who has no place to lay his head save the meagre shelter afforded by some covered truck or the scanty refuge of some dark and damp passageway.

GROPING IN THE DARK.

One of my companions who entered another lodging house related the following to me :—

"We arrived at the stoop of the dark entrance to the long, narrow passage leading to what I supposed to be the office in which I should see the landlord, with whom I would make all arrangements. We opened the door and walked in without any ceremony, but I found that we were mistaken—that it was a room occupied by tenants. I say tenants in the plural, for there was a whole family—father, mother and several children—that lived, ate, drank and slept all in that one small room—only a room about 16 by 18 feet. Everything looked dirty, loathsome and repulsive. We asked if the 'boss' was in.

"'Noo, up stairs,' grunted the grizzly looking being that was sitting on a stool sucking a dirty clay pipe. We turned from this sight and from the foul air of the room, forgetting to close the door as we departed.

"The man at once picked up a lump of coal and with an oath wildly hurled it at us.

"We then groped our way through the dark up the stairs, and at last discovered a doorway, at which we knocked.

"A young man responded, and demanded what we wished. We said we wanted a place to sleep.

He replied, 'We have not got room.'

But a feminine voice behind answered, 'There is room upstairs.'

So, with an old lamp, he led us up another flight, and knocked at the first door he came to.

"There was no response. He commenced to kick at the door. Still no response, save the cursings, which could be heard from other portions of the house. He swore, adding, 'I'll smash the d——d thing in !' whereupon he lifted his foot and began kicking violently, and then put his shoulder against it in an effort to force it open.

"Then a perfect pandemonium reigned. Men and women commenced calling, groaning and shouting, 'Let us sleep.' He paid no attention to them, and, while still pressing against the door, it was suddenly opened from within.

A NIGHT IN A BUNK.

"Here we found a crowded bedroom. Our bunks were

allotted us. My companion only removed his overcoat, and
then rolled in. I hesitated for twenty minutes. The bed-
clothing was dirty, and to use my comrade's expression,
'rotten.' At last I sprang up, lying in my clothes. Oh, what
a night of moral as well as literal darkness was that to scores
of people around us in that overcrowded building! I overheard the low and vicious conversation through the thin
partition of two of the occupants, a man and a woman, in the
next room. On the floor above was another woman, whose
voice seemed to indicate old age. She mixed, in a foul and
dazed manner, religion with obscenity, and then broke out
with the sentence, 'I'll stand up for the captain of The Salvation Army.'

"Evidently the slum women in visiting this low quarter
were recognized as doing a mission that called forth the
gratitude of this poor, drink-crazed mind. After a few
moments of silence I heard shrieks and oaths and curses.
Two women had descended the stairs and gone to the hydrant
outside to draw some water at the same time, and were in
hot dispute as to who had the first claim. They quarreled,
and then vile language followed such as I could never repeat.

"I tossed about in my hard bunk. It was dark. The door
was fast! The place was stifling! But a worse experience
than all previous ones followed. I soon became conscious of
the fact that the room was not only dirty, but was overrun
with vermin, and then a fuller horror of our situation seized
me.

"What was I to do? I lay longing for the dawn of day,
and I do not think I slept more than one hour. I arose as the
first streak of morning light fell into the room, and made my
way down out of the wretched building, bringing with me a
recollection of the first night in a New York lodging house
that I do not think time will ever erase."

Here is the experience of another lodging house that was tried, and the testimony of a poor unsheltered man concern. ing the place :—

We went up into the office to pay for our tickets, and as we stepped up to give our ten cents we stumbled over several men lying on the floor near the stove in a dark room. It was filthy, and covered with tobacco juice. The man in charge

"NO THANKS ; I WAS THERE THREE WEEKS AGO."

did not give us our tickets immediately, but merely registered our Christian names, and led us up another flight of stairs. We then entered a room where there were forty men lying in bunks, one close above another; the atmosphere was filled with the smell of vile tobacco, drink and that almost un. bearable odor coming from the herding of many men together whose personal habits are filthy. The men themselves were almost stripped, and their clothes thrown about in heaps in all directions. We couldn't remain in so filthy a place.

A FIVE-CENT DOUBLE DECKER.

We returned down stairs, secured our tickets from the man in charge, and had hardly reached the sidewalk before

we met a man whose appearance bespoke utter destitution
and poverty. We inquired of him as to how he was fixed up
for the night. He said he expected to walk the streets all
night, and we at once handed him one of the tickets.

He eagerly took it, and looked at the number; then to our
surprise immediately handed it back, saying, "No, thank you;
I am clean now, and that is a filthy, lousy place."

We asked him how long he had been without employment
and a place to sleep. He replied, "For two weeks." We then
inquired whether he drank. He said that he had sworn off at
Christmas, and that he had not touched a drop of liquor since
then. We then asked whether as soon as he had found employment he would turn to drink again. He answered with
a ring of sincerity that he had made up his mind that he
would never touch another drop of beer, supplementing his
answer with an oath.

We then inquired, "What is your nationality?" He
answered, "I am an American."

"So am I," my companion replied; "give me your hand."

He said that he had been in search of work for two months,
and that he had nothing but an occasional job of cleaning
sidewalks. He explained in sad and despairing tones that he
had remained in mission halls and Salvation Army barracks
until half-past ten and eleven o'clock, and had then to turn
out to walk the cold and pitiless streets penniless and homeless
all night. Let it be remembered that he thought that those
to whom he was speaking were such as himself.

We talked on while we stood close to the lodging house
which, before he would enter, he vowed he would rather
walk till his overtired body dropped. "I am clean," he said,
"if nothing else. I was there one night three weeks ago, and
I was covered with filth and vermin, and I swore I'd never
cross its doors again,"

Before leaving him we dealt with him about his soul, but received the answer, "I don't have much time to think about it; it keeps a fellow always going to keep one's body alive."

We bid our new acquaintance good-bye, and ah! how loth we were to leave him to the mercy of the cold and heartless night; how we wished our Salvation Army Shelters were opened, and that we had some warm, comfortable place to which we could have invited this poor, unbefriended fellow countryman !

GIVING AWAY A LODGING TICKET—"TANKE, SIR !"

We jostled along a little further until we ran across an

aged and crippled man. I wish our plentifully clothed fellow citizens could have looked but for a few moments upon that dejected and pitiful object. A few loose and foul rags hung from his bent and crippled frame. His hair was long and matted and his face sunken and depraved.

We stopped, and holding out the ticket as we touched him on the arm, we said, "Would you like a place to sleep to-night?" He looked at us with an incredulous stare and stammered, hardly above a whisper, "No." Then he clutched it with his skeleton hand and, chuckling for a moment, shuffled on faster out of sight.

CHAPTER III.

OPIUM HAUNTS AND RESORTS OF THIEVES.

THE next streets up which we passed were exceptionally close, with high buildings containing small windows and many entrances on either side. There were very narrow and miserably paved sidewalks.

"What quarter is this?" I asked of one of my companions as I drew nearer to him.

"Speak a little lower," he replied. "This is the Chinese quarter, and perhaps the worst portion of that quarter," and surely it was hardly necessary for him to inform me of this, for the next moment we were pretty well surrounded with the fluttering gowns of passing members of the community that represents the Celestial Empire.

Stop! Do you see those coils of smoke? Look down those stone steps. See that form—that silent being bent over that small light! And see how dexterously and care-fully that hand turns round the small glutinous substance at the end of that long needle. What is it that makes those eyes brighten for a few moments, and absorbs the attention of the individual looking toward the point of that needle? What is it causes his eyes to dilate with expectation? *Opium.* And hundreds of 'women in this city before this night is past will have allowed themselves to come beneath its baneful, demoralizing influence.

I could not help but wish that a similar work could be commenced among the Chinese portion of this city as that being prosecuted by our indefatigable workers in that section inhabited by the Chinese in the city of Melbourne, Victoria, Australia, where to my knowledge a good work has been accomplished.

We wended our way next to Mulberry Street, the haunt of desperadoes.

We reached there a little before midnight—truly the devil's midday in this benighted and drink-cursed quarter. Here we found crowds upon both sidewalks who were holding high carnival. The incessant swinging of saloon doors which

AN OPIUM JOINT

admitted customers to hot and fetid rooms where the worst kind of liquor is sold, was conspicuous on all sides. One had at times to literally push one's way through the uncouth, vicious-looking men, and past low women utterly lost to all virtue and sense of goodness.

WHERE IT WAS DANGEROUS TO SPEAK.

The number of lighted windows on either side, story above story, showed that there was life within, and that instead of

the residents being asleep they were taking part in the dark
revelry, actuated by the same spirit that prompted the hearts
of those who were slaves to drink and debauchery without.

We walked on to the place, of which one of my companions said :—

"Perhaps more crimes have been perpetrated and murders
committed here than on any other one spot in the dark
city."

We had no detectives or protection with us save that un-
seen. I buttoned my ragged coat closer round my neck, and
drew my old hat lower over my face.

ROBBING A DRUNKEN MAN.

"Do not speak loud," said my companion, and I walked on
silently along what I believe is one of the worst neighborhoods I ever trod, and a foul blot upon the good name of our
fair country. I can understand one writing of this neighborhood saying there is not a sin in the decalogue but flourishes
in this quarter, for if the stones could speak, then each would

have to record some dark and bloody deed committed within
the circle of that fever-stricken and pestilential place.

We had not walked far before the loud and rapid utter-
ances of an Italian caused us to stop on the outskirts of a
small crowd. It was dark, but by the dim light of a flickering
lamp we could see the outline of a strong and tall man, who
was being held back by one of his own sex, while a woman
hung on each arm, frustrating his efforts to attack a woman.

It was the woman's attitude that particularly arrested
our attention—a woman with set lips and brazen expression
holding up a brawny arm and clenched hand. They drew
nearer to each other, and I could see the bruise upon her
forehead, and the plaster that hid another wound upon the
side of her face. A torrent of language followed, and then a
shuffle, and the Italian was drawn back into the shadow of
saloon, for two policemen carrying their long night clubs had
arrived upon the spot. For us to stand any longer was only
to create suspicion, and we moved on.

A TOUCH ON THE ARM.

A few paces further and I felt some one suddenly clutch
my arm. I looked around, at the same moment shrinking
back a step.

Who could it be? No one knew me in this of all places on
earth.

Who was it—it was a woman—one of those dissipated
creatures who carry the brand given by society all through
their downward career to the grave of despair and death. I
looked into her face for a few seconds, and then forcibly with-
drawing my arm I turned and without saying a word passed
along into the crowd saddened at heart.

It was an awful place. I had heard our slum sisters speak
of the misery, of the benighted homes, of the woebegone

creatures who lived in them, but here I was right in the heart of the seething evil and curse, and for once I myself was looking into the faces of those into whose life scarce a spark of joy or a ray of hope dawns, except the mocking mirth that comes from hell and the tantalizing hope that is never realized.

A SCENE OF SQUALOR.

The following scene of wretchedness is but one of the many our officers witness in this neighborhood :—

"Up three broad steps, and we are in a large, wide passage, which has evidently seen very much better days. On the door hangs a white drapery; some little one is dead. The dejected form of a woman leans against the wall, apparently with no aim, no wish, in an attitude of deepest dejection. We ask her what she is watching for. Lifting her heavy eyelids, she looks at us in a sullen, almost stupid manner, but all we can get from her is, 'Waiting for the funeral; waiting for the funeral!' and those swollen eyelids fall again.

"We leave her, and mounting the stairs, enter a little, dark room, almost entirely devoid of furniture. We pass through it to the one in the rear. It also is very small. In the centre on a table lies the form of a dead babe, its mother and a neighbor sitting on one side.

"This is what first meets our gaze, but as our eyes get accustomed to the dim light from the one candle burning on the brass chandelier, we see there are others in the room. On the right hand side is an old lounge, and on it lie what at first seem to be two bundles. They are the two little brothers of the dead baby; one, as we lean over and look into his thin, pale little face, with sunken eyes and bloodless lips, looks as if he must soon have to follow baby. Both are just huddled up, with their ragged coats on, trying to keep warm. Two little girls look wistfully up into our faces from the

other side of the room, then climb on a chair and look at the
still, cold face of the one they, though so tiny themselves,
had often nursed and tried to soothe.   But now our eyes fall
on the saddest part of that picture.   The father of these children lies in a drunken stupor in the other corner of the room.
All goodness and manliness gone, there he lay like a log, un-
conscious of anything—drunk, drunk ! And yet the wife
tried to shield him, saying that he had sat up with them two
nights, and was so tired ! She then got up to put the shoes
we had brought for the babe upon its little feet. What a
shocking sight that poor little creature's legs presented—
white, yellowish skin hanging on long, straight bones, with
a slight enlargement which marked where the knee came—
and nothing more !

"We talked to them, prayed with them, and, promising
to come again, began to make our way toward the door,
when the great, heavy form of the 'father' slowly rolled over
and rose, to reel round once or twice, stagger into the next
room and, fortunately, sink into a chair, where we were
obliged to leave him, and leave them to him and—God."

Some distance further, after we had turned into an off
street, we saw a motley crowd gathered around a dark doorway.   Then the door suddenly opened and a woman stepped
out on to the sidewalk and beckoned with her bony finger to
a policeman. He stepped up, struck a match, walked in and
closed the door behind him. Then we heard a slight scuffle
within and a shuffling of feet.

We waited some seconds, or, I should have said, we did
not go away, but moved about so as to avoid any suspicion.
Then the door opened and two men, whom I judged from
their dress to be detectives, held on either arm a poor, helpless, besotted drunkard. He was an old man with sunken

cheeks and torn and filthy rags covered his emaciated body.

"Get up," said one of the policemen, using his long night club. The man's head dropped, his form leaned forward and his feet fell from under him. In this condition, murmuring to himself half aloud, he was carried off by the detectives to the police station.

Not a nightly occurrence only, nay an hourly, an almost momentary occurrence in these dark haunts of the great city.

"Come on," I said to my companion, "I have seen enough."

A WAIF OF THE STREETS.

SALOONS IN LEGIONS.

But the saloons—how many were there? Hundreds. In

Cherry street alone, along one side of that street only, we counted twenty-seven in three blocks. And mind you, almost every saloon was crowded with customers, the majority of whom were either drinking, shouting, cursing or swearing.

I have been told that there are thirty thousand saloons in New York City. I thought the statement one that should have little credence. But after passing up street after street in which almost every second or third house was one of those polling houses to destruction and ruin I can no longer doubt the statement.

I and my comrades decided to count the number of drunken individuals who passed us during that night, and within three hours we counted not less than fifty-five persons. who were so far intoxicated as to be unable to walk straight upon the sidewalk, and this number was exclusive of those we counted within saloons, and in some we found as many as five, six, ten and even fifteen.

Let any one who is disposed to think me over-estimating the number of these resorts or coloring my description of the blight and curse they occasion walk along the Bowery on Saturday night between the hours of ten and twelve, and if he be unmoved by the scores of pitiful objects and woebegone creatures who will pass him within an hour he must surely possess an adamantine heart.

CHAPTER IV.

EVER MOVING ON AIMLESSLY.

IT is growing colder, and the wind blows sharper and keener. A glance through the large, brightly polished windows of the saloons tells us that the hand has reached the figure twelve on the dial of the clock. There is a sudden exit of men and women from these liquor rooms, and a closing and locking of their doors. A large theatre is just emptying itself, and crowds of men and women are flocking past us on either side.

"Now," said my comrade, who had spent some years in the very neighborhood through which I was walking, "you have been told that there are few men who have to walk about this great city without home or shelter. But what you will see will prove a very different experience from what you have heard."

We walked a little more briskly, though tired and languid. And, besides, it is between the hours of twelve and four that one standing or lurking about is liable to be seized by the strong arm of the law for vagrancy, and having no credentials upon us and only a few cents in our pockets we thought it wise to keep "on the move."

The Latin proverb reads, "The silent features have often both words and expressions of their own." True! And the faces of the men who passed us, looking well-nigh numb with cold. and with haggard and gaunt expressions, spoke infinitely more than words of the wretched and shelterless night that lay before them.

" But it is after twelve o'clock," I said to my companion ; " what are all these men doing at this hour walking about ? "

Tramp, tramp, tramp, to the right and left of us, with their hands tucked in their sleeves and their heads bent as though they were looking upon the sidewalk for some less hard place than the pitiless stones beneath them to lay their weary, aching bones upon.

" Will not these men have some place to sleep to-night ? " I inquired.

" No, sir," replied my companion. " I have been one of them myself, and have wandered the streets regularly for nights. Let me take you to the streets where they sleep upon the wagons and trucks. Do you see that covered truck there? I slept in that very truck for two nights. I would have slept there longer but for being disturbed by the police. You should come down here some wet night and see some of these men creeping under steps and into dark passageways and under trucks and wagons for some shelter from the rain and protection from the wind. Ah, sir, it would make your heart ache."

POVERTY, THEN CRIME.

On we sped, still passing scores of men, some of them young men, apparently strong and capable of work.

Do you say they were thieves ?

I answer emphatically, " No !."

Possibly one in every six may have been a character rightly designated by such a description, but the mass of these men my companion (who had spent the blackest and most miserable part of his life within this precinct) assured me were men who had no work, no purse to pay for a shelter, and no roof beneath which to lay their heads.

Speak to that man standing at that street corner. Talk to

him about means. Why, he has not the miserable pittance
that would pay for a night's lodging. There is not a dime on
his person. He will look you in the face and say:

"Give me work, and then talk about money. Give me
a chance to earn some food, and then talk about paying
for it."

Some of our field officers have spoken to these men concerning their future, have urged them in loving and earnest

THE FIGHT IN FRONT OF THE DIVE.

terms to live a better life and prepare for death, and while
conversing with them have been forced to say mentally,
"This man already experiences the existence of a living
death. He lacks food, and we have need to give him the
physical bread before talking to him of the spiritual."

What is to be done with these out-of-works?

What ought to be done for these men who spend these nights in the cold, in the storm, unsought, unhoused, unbefriended ?

It is these very men we seek to help and for whom we propose to open shelter houses where they can receive food for the body—plain, good, substantial food—and after supplying their bodily wants, we propose to bring them within the influence of that grace which will supply their spiritual needs.

It is the welfare of these men that I feel unutterably concerned about. By helping, reclaiming and saving one of these men I add another good member to society, and I better the condition of the community. I strengthen its safety and lessen its dangers, and, after all, "it is the welfare of the people that is the supreme law."

It may be asked, "Ought not the police to interfere and prevent them sleeping out of doors?"

Let me assure my readers that the police have more now than they can possibly do, and the courts, too, for that matter. The officers of the law have again and again assured me that their time is almost wholly absorbed in looking after these poor unfortunates.

What is wanted is more suitable and efficient accommodation, more comfortable and inviting shelter for these men who are not only, and for some time have not only been, out of work, but whose efforts to obtain work have been fruitless.

CHAPTER V.

HOW TO SAVE THE SUFFERERS.

THERE is another phase to this great city life, and one which cannot be overlooked, and that is the daily trapping of the victims who have dropped into its whirlpool from country life—innocent and unsophisticated young men, who tramp the streets to find a lodging, and then are herded in with those who are already as bad as human beings can well-nigh be out of hell.

In many instances they have fallen to moral, aye, and to social depths before they have time to realize their surroundings and appreciate any remedy.

Repeatedly the girls who have talked to our Slum sisters in the dives and drinking saloons have said that they had no idea of the place they were coming to, and that the father or mother, far away in the country, knows nothing about it either ; that they are hopeless and despairing, and brushing away the tears, they whirl back into the dance, and seem to toss down glasses of spirits to try to blunt the edge of their misery and shame.

Few places can exert a wider or more harmful influence than the large building, to the threshold of which I threaded my way, on the Bowery, the name of which I withhold, but which, with others, is made conspicuous by a notice outside that is deceptive in its character. It is an open auditorium, fitted up with tables, to and from which waiters are ever hurrying with wine and spirits.

I, of course, was not allowed to enter. I was looked upon as altogether too poverty-stricken and dejected to cross its threshold, over which a stream of humanity was incessantly pouring. My companion turned and whispered to me that hundreds in this and like buildings received the first deadly poison that devours and destroys both body and soul.

Further along, on the opposite side of the same street, was another building, at the doors of which a man, dressed up in a manner calculated to arouse the curiosity of passers-by, was calling out at the top of his voice :—"Step inside ; Step inside ! Seats all free ! All seats free !" One glance within revealed a large room, theatre-like in size and circus-like in shape. The air was filled with clouds of the coveted weed and the strong odor of drink.

DRINK, ONLY DRINK.

I stopped at the doorway a few moments and glanced around. Men were rushing about from seat to seat and table to table with bottles of all colors bearing foreign labels. Drink !

It was all drink.

It was drink at every turn, whichever way one cast one's eyes. This seemed the one indispensable source to which the thief, the harlot, the criminal and the murderer turned. If strength was needed for the weak frame, if nerve required for the daring deed, if solace wanted for some troubled breast, it could be obtained at the same fiery source—*drink !*

The fact that alcohol destroys 100,000 lives in this country annually, that it makes 70,000 widows and throws 100,000 orphans upon our hands ; that it causes 500 maniacs and as many suicides, and consigns to our jails some 500,000 crimi-nals, had no particle of weight with these heedless, reckless souls.

They wanted pleasure ; they only sought to appease their lower appetites in sin and debauchery. On they swept to drink deeper from the stream, the waters of which carry putrefaction and death.

But I had seen enough, and turning to my companions I said, "Let us leave and go home." Ah! welcome word. For but for the grace of God we, as others who walked with heavy and tired feet on either side of us, might have been homeless, without bread and without that for which we now can gladly sacrifice bread, the life that never dies, and without which the soul has but the fearful looking forward to of the death that never ends.

One more look, which brought in its turn such pity as I have rarely before experienced for those whose only cathedrals are the cold and miserable streets of this great city. Though I had seen with my own eyes so many different aspects of the city life, yet this was the one all absorbing phase —the need of hands of rescue, homes of refuge for these unpitied, unreached, unhoused and unchurched fellow-citizens.

Oh, that anything I might say might arouse the sympathies of those who have wealth and influence at their command by which they can succor and uplift these hungry and weird-looking men who tramp the streets of our Empire City!

AND WHAT IS THE REMEDY?

Right thankful was I to again reach our Headquarters on Reade Street, where I changed my disheveled and tattered clothes for my Army uniform.

Still more gratitude did I experience when reaching the stoop of my own home, and though my dear wife at the same time had been visiting, in company with the Slum sisters, other haunts and centres of vice and sin, taking hope and peace with her to the hopeless and peaceless, and was still absent, yet I did not grudge an hour of her time—for was it not that for which I had just been wishing? And in the stead of that one woman, and in the place of that small brigade of Slum angels, I could have wished that a thousand ladies of New York City could have entered the homes, unadorned by purity and unknown to peace, and that a thousand men, whose hearts are touched by the love of humanity, could be scattered among their disheartened and despairing fellow-citizens.

Will this day dawn—this day that shall bring joy to these heavy hearts and brightness to these darkened souls?

Oh, that God, who looks down upon the tangled maze of human affairs with infinite love and pity, may cause the uprising of those touched with the love that filled and inspired the breast of the Saviour of Nazareth—the Friend of the poor, who was not ashamed to eat with publicans and sinners—that they may become helpers and saviours of mankind!

MRS. BOOTH'S DISCOVERIES.

PATHOS AND TRAGEDY ENCOUNTERED IN A NIGHT TOUR WITH SALVATION GIRLS.

AM weary and stiff and my head aches from the sights and sounds, the darkness and the horror of the last twenty-four hours.

But my heart aches far more than my body, and I feel the crushing and weary burden that I always experience when I step back into life from the darkness of death and damnation of New York's hell.

I do not see how any woman whose heart is capable of feeling—any mother, any wife—could go into this darkness and come out the same as she entered. I feel years older! But, ah! how powerless are lips to describe or pens to write scenes which baffle description and which no ink is black enough to show in their true colors.

What can I say? How can I begin? And how can I ever hope to make others see these things as we have seen them?

It is indeed a hopeless task.   But if a brief chronicle of
the last twenty-four hours can convey even a vague idea of
Slumdom and of the life work of our slum saviours, I will
gladly jot down the lights and shadows of last night as they
pass again in panorama before my mind.

CHAPTER VI.

HEART CHILLED FROM THE START.

IT was chilly. Evening was falling. The pale yellow sunset made the muddy streets and lengthening shadows all the drearier, and the biting frost made us wrap our shawls close around us as we hurried from Headquarters toward the East side slums. My ragged calico-wrapper flapped drearily in the wind and the mud splashed round us at every step.

Already an oppressive sense of that which would have to be faced during the next few hours made me feel sad and weary. And everything around us seemed so cheerless that we shivered at the thought of what that night's frost would, mean to the hundreds of homeless ones among whom we were going to work.

Cherry Hill and its surroundings presented a picture of busy, hurrying life.

It was Saturday night, and quarreling women; squalid children, tired men and dissipated boys jostled confusedly along the sidewalks. The streets were like rivers of black mud, through which one had to wade on the uneven cobble-stones, stepping from one little, comparatively dry island to another and alternately sinking ankle deep in the filth. Heaps of rubbish, numberless wooden hoops broken off beer casks and refuse of every description ornamented the road-way.

We passed quickly through the throng, recognized on every hand with "Good evening, sister !" "Oh ! there are the Salvation girls !" "Good evening !" "Good evening !"

cheerily came from the women standing gossiping on their
stoops, and from the policeman on the corner watching suspiciously the actions of the many ragged ones already be-

MRS. BOOTH IN SLUMMING COSTUME.

coming quarrelsome in preparation for Saturday night brawls
that make the night lively throughout this precinct.

We turned quickly into our little Slum quarters to be

greeted by the bright faces of the five Slum girls living there and working lovingly and patiently under the direction of my brave companion, Staff-Capt. Bown. We paused but a few moments to talk together, and then I slipped up stairs to the nursery to see the sleeping babies, whose weary mothers would soon come to fetch them after their day's work was done.

INSPECTING SLUM NURSERY BABIES.

Bright and cheery and clean looked the little room, and peaceful looked the little white faces of the sleeping babies. In the hammock swung a six-weeks-old little one, with its blue eyes staring contentedly up at the ceiling. On the rocking chair by the fire was a tiny girl. Two years of age she was said to be; but, oh, how thin and wan was her little face, and how bony her tiny fingers as she clasped them and rocked quietly to and fro.

Then I was taken into the inner room—the sleeping-room —and there in their little cots three more little ones were sleeping. The light streamed down from the window upon the face of one; and as I lifted the little red blanket back and looked at the tiny face there was perfect contentment written there, although the little one in the few months of his life had seen sickness and sorrow, want and hunger.

But I quickly put the blanket back and crept away on hearing that this was the most fretful and troublesome baby of the lot, fearing to waken and call him back from dreamland to the world which worries and ruffles so much his poor little temper. I turned to another cot where a six-weeks-old baby was waking.

Lovingly he was taken up in the arms of one of the Slum girls, and a smile flickered on his baby face. Poor little one! His mother brought him there hopeless and despairing a few mornings since. She was told she could not leave him on ac-

HOMELESS BOYS IN THE LUMBER PILES.

count of sickness in the nursery, and with the tears coursing down her wan cheeks she told of her misery.

SAVED FROM DESPAIR.

No home, no friend to turn to, no night's lodging, no food to eat for four and twenty hours! And, alas! no work to be obtained with that little one in her arms. She pleaded very pitifully for her little one to be cared for while she went out to try and find work, and added :—

"I am so wretched I feel tempted to cut my throat. For what can I do? What can I do?"

So the baby had been cared for during the day, and she comes for him at night—not knowing where she can find a shelter for him and herself, and they go out together into the chilly night, homeless and desolate; but she presses him to her mother's heart and feels comforted.

We came down again and asked a few questions as to the visits of the day, and then we hurried out into the chilly streets.

It was even colder now. The sunset had flickered out and darkness had fallen. Ah! well it had, for surely it was a fit pall to cover the living death of vice which held high carnival.

One of the first sights that met us as we crossed the street was the figure of a tiny boy stooping over something spilled upon the sidewalk. He had been sent out for a few cents' worth of groceries; a string had given way and a package opening at both ends had let out a brown stream of coffee which was mixing with the mud. Sitting down upon a step he looked in dismay at the broken package, big tears rolled down his white cheeks and a howl of utter desolation broke forth. Poor little fellow! He could not have been more than five years old!

SOOTHING A CHILD'S GRIEF.

Instantly my companion sat down upon the muddy step
with him, and stopping the escaping coffee, folded the paper
and carefully arranged the little package, while I untied the
string to fasten it for her. He looked up with blue eyes full
of surprise, and the lamplight flickered in the big tears ready
to drop, but checked by wonder. In a few minutes a crowd
of boys had gathered round us.

THE WAIFS SLEEPING UNDER A WAGON.

"What's the matter here?" shouted one to the other.

"Oh, it's the Salvation sisters picking up that shaver's
coffee for him."

A dirty, mischievous hand grabbed some of that which
had already been trodden into the mud.

"Get back, you!" shouted another urchin. "What do
yer want to steal the bloke's coffee for?"

"Oh!" exclaimed a third, "that's what the sisters are
doing!"

"No, they ain't! They don't steal nothing. They ain't
thieves, like you!" came back the answer.

The little package was fastened up by now and securely stowed away in a pocket of the little fellow's ragged jacket, and he trotted away through the crowd homeward bound, but fortunately saved from the warm welcome which doubtless would have greeted him.

TYING UP THE COFFEE.

CHAPTER VII.

WHERE POVERTY ABIDES ALWAYS.

WE hurried away in the opposite direction, for time flies and we were bound for an hour or so of visiting before supper. We turned in at a door upon which there may once have been a bell, but no bell-ringing or knocking was necessary now, for it is one of the poorest lodging houses of the city—only *one* of them. Would to God it were the *only* one! But there are many, many more just like it.

An old man paused as we passed in, his tattered hat drawn over his face, which bore unmistakably the marks of sickness and vice. As he saw us a smile flickered round his otherwise grim mouth, and he greeted my companion warmly.

We passed on, up one flight of dirty stairs, the boards of which creaked ominously beneath us. A fusty, stifling smell made us hold our breath. Another flight—the air became fouler. We paused for a moment's rest upon the landing. There was a large ash barrel already full of refuse! Another flight—it grew darker, and the gaslight below became indistinct. Yet another flight, and now the smell became a perfect stench, and we had carefully to feel our way along in the dusk. There was but a flickering of faint light below us as we waited upon another landing.

All the doors were closed, but we could hear the sound of brawling and fighting within. Before us was a door to which we groped our way, and then began to ascend the garret stairs. Then we were in pitch blackness—not a glimmer of light—and the air seemed about as thick as the

56

darkness around us. The stairs were very narrow and we had to feel our way by the wall as we mounted.

At last we had reached the top of the house. No light of any description was there. The eaves of the house fell low all around us, and although it was too dark to see them, bare rafters were over our heads. There was a door in front of us; we heard talking, and stepping up to it, we knocked.

ABODE OF THE DRINK RIDDEN.

" Who's there?" shouted a voice, and unbidden we opened the door. Directly my companion was seen and The Army badge upon her old gray shawl recognized we were gladly bidden to enter. The room was lighted by a lamp, the glass of which was smoked and broken, and had been patched with brown paper. In front of us stood an old woman in a tattered black dress, her already gray hair matted and disordered and her face bloated. At the table a man was working, who took absolutely no notice of our entrance, and on the only other chair visible sat an old woman with a market basket in her hands—evidently a neighbor.

My companion was no stranger in the room, and she began at once to talk gently and in a neighborly way with the woman, who is a hard drinker, and yet who has a heart capable of being touched with a desire to do better. My companion sat down upon an old box and I was most cordially invited to sit down upon the bed. My heart sank just a little lower as I did so. Bed clothing—at least as we are accustomed to speak of it—there was none; but an old quilt or comfort was spread over the mattress, and I saw enough at one glance to make me turn away and try to forget that I had taken my seat there.

I watched the flickering of the lamplight on the two faces—one so pure and good, the other so bloated and sin

PRAYING IN A FAMILY LODGING HOME—SIX FAMILIES IN ONE ROOM.

spoiled. My companion was pleading with her patiently, lovingly; trying to get the truth into her poor, befogged mind ; and while they talked I glanced around the room.

It was a very small garret apartment ; the beams ran low and there was no pretence at paint or plaster. In every direction the walls and ceilings were draped with cobwebs. It looked as if hundreds of busy spiders had been at work for generations past. Across the window an old rag hung which might possibly be dignified by the name of curtain. We could hear the sound of shouting and riot in the streets, and I wondered why it was so distinct—as the window did not seem made to open, and then I noticed that some panes were gone, and the cold night air—proving a blessing in disguise—could be felt through the otherwise stifling atmosphere.

TOUCHED UNTO TEARS.

" Will you sing to me ?" I heard the woman say, and then all was still while we sang :—

Your garments must be white as snow,
Prepare to meet your God.
For to His throne we all must go,
Prepare to meet thy God.
Prepare me, prepare me, Lord, to stand before Thy Throne.

I watched the change upon her face ; tears welled up into her eyes, and then slowly coursed down her cheeks. We knelt down to pray, and then turned away from the wretched room where drink had made such havoc, feeling thankful that song and prayer could still touch this heart so hardened to all else.

Out on the landing again in the dark of night we groped our way across to another door and knocked. No response but the sound of loud quarreling within. We knocked again. Fumes of tobacco smoke had found their way through the chinks in the door and made the air still more difficult to breathe. We knocked louder in desperation, anxious to get in out of the darkness.

At last the door opened, and we asked if there was not a sick woman there. "Yes," and we were bidden welcome.

Oh, it seems impossible to describe this room! Could I paint it in all its desolation and filth, with the sad, dark colors it would need, my picture would be styled exaggerated. But without any hesitation I can say that there was no room for exaggeration, for imagination could depict nothing worse.

POVERTY BEYOND DESCRIPTION.

The room was chilly and damp, and one shuddered as if entering a vault. The uneven and rotten boards of the floor were black with layers of dirt, and the roof, which was composed only of rafters, was ceiled with deposits of dirt, cobweb and soot. Especially over the corner where the stove had been the soot was so thick that it hung in black layers and flakes. The window was broken, and to replace the many missing panes rags had been hung over it and propped up with a piece of kindling wood. The room was utterly devoid of furniture. There was but one chair, but that stood away in a corner, with the back long since broken off and the bottom gone. It consisted simply of legs!

There was a shaky wooden bench, and to this, with an apology for its poor accommodation, we were invited with a touch of gallantry by a poor, tottering, drunken man, who knew the slum saviours well enough to show them respect.

The bedstead was an iron one, but through age it had given way in the middle. A few rags were all the bed covering of which it could boast, and in the midst' of them, emaciated by sickness and pinched by hunger, with her hair already whitened by age, and limbs shivering in the bitter cold, sat a sick woman. Her only garment was a torn waist, which she tried to hold around her with thin, bony hands.

"Yes, she has been feeling very sick. She is sick all the time now." But she asked eagerly how the two sick slum

"COME ALONG, SIS."

officers were, and said that she had been thinking of them.

Her husband sat at the foot of the bed and tried to talk to us, but he was incoherent and rambling, excited one minute, despairing the next. A little of his story I have learned, and it is but the story of hundreds more.

A TYPICAL STORY.

No work, weary tramps and endless searching, and yet still no work ; companions who would offer him drink and he (starving and despairing) takes it, and there is nothing else ; returning at night, tired and footsore, he has to sit up by a groaning wife in a cheerless, cold room with nothing to give her to eat, and to fall asleep knowing that there is no better hope on the waking to-morrow.

He had been several times to the slum quarters—not to beg nor to borrow—only to say how sick he was of his own wretched efforts to do better, and to be prayed with. A very independent nature, so they told me, with some fine touches and traits in his character, which make it impossible for him to be a beggar, though hunger and misery are his daily companions.

But to return to the room. One thing I have left un-mentioned. It is a broken stove filled with gray ashes, but no sign of fire. A crust lay on the table and a little salt was in a plate ; but they had had nothing to eat that day, and there was no hope of anything to eat on the next.

"But on Monday," he said, "the old woman shall have all she wants, for I am going to work "—hope was not yet gone!

A little inner room or cupboard I noticed at the end of this room. It was another apartment let separately to another lodger, with room only for a bed, and I could hear sounds which came from the drunken woman who occupied this garret corner. The whole scene was depressing, and the icy coldness of the room made the filth and stench all the more horrible

SICKNESS BEYOND HOPE.

The sick woman had a wound several inches deep upon

her leg, inflicted, I afterwards learned, by a quarrelsome neighbor. But that which caused her suffering and weariness and loss of sleep and the groans which broke from her as she moved, was a dread disease whose grip she will never more shake off.

Great knotted lumps were upon her breast, and as she told us the doctor said this would all have to be cut out, the word "cancer" flashed through our minds. That is why she would not go to a hospital, because she feared to face this operation. She was sure she would never live through it. But as we looked around at the misery, and thought of the starvation and cold and loneliness, we felt that the living death was worse than dying—were it not for the hereafter.

All this time my companion had been talking faithfully to the drunken man, and I heard him cursing the drink and telling her how he hated it—telling her that could the dead mother of the beautiful French home of years ago see him now she would never know him—never! never! She would not believe her son could fall so low or reach that wretched garret.

Then we knelt down beside the bed and prayed to the One whose eyes can see through the darkness and wretchedness into those desolate hearts. And as we prayed the woman rocked to and fro sobbing, and the man responded, "Yes, yes; that's true! My God, help me!" while the tears washed his unwashed face and he pushed his fingers through his matted hair.

Then we took leave, promising to send some toast and a cup of tea to the sick one.

The door was left open so that we could grope our way across the passage, and we began to descend into the darkness of the narrow stairway. My companion went first, and as I

followed her into the shadows I looked back across the landing and I shall not forget that last look. I could no longer
see the occupants of the room—merely the end of the old
bedstead—but their shadows were cast upon the wall! The
woman was still sitting up in bed, with her long, bony
fingers beckoning to her husband, as she tried to rouse him
from his drunken stupor and shouted :—

"Can't you light the ladies down? Can't you hold a lamp
for 'em?" The back shadows were standing out on the wall
in bold relief, and the weak voice, querulous and shrill, gave
the scene a weird aspect.

"SAY, SING FOR US."

CHAPTER VIII.

FROM SHADOW TO BLACKNESS.

THEN we entered into the blackness again, and found ourselves presently upon the landing below. Turning into another room for a short call, we were welcomed and told of the family's welfare—or ill-fare it would be probably better to say—and where we listened to the violent rating at the husband from his wife because he had neglected to offer us a seat.

"Oh! it's a poor welcome you give the ladies, Mike, if yer can't have the common dacency to show 'em to a seat!"

But Mike was not concerned, and just then was engrossed in talking out his troubles to my companion, who sympathized with him over a pair of spectacles which he had recently purchased, but which did not assist his failing sight.

Then down the stairs again we went and entered a room in which we found six double beds. No partitions, no screens; families living here, too, huddled together in one common room. Here the cooking, washing, sleeping was all done. Fighting, living and dying went on—sometimes all at the same time. Its windows only let in the light and air when broken, and the air was so thick with tobacco smoke that we could hardly breathe. Men, women and children drag out a miserable existence in this place. The bed nearest the door had a string across the top of it and some filthy rags hung over it.

BABY'S LONG WAIT FOR MAMMA.

It was the first thing that attracted my attention, for over the rags peered a golden head of a perfect little angel. True, the tiny face was dirty, and the mass of golden curls was tangled, but it was a strikingly beautiful child, and such a contrast to the rags around the bed on which it crouched. The little dress it wore was insufficient to cover it and had slipped down over the baby shoulders, and I saw the skin was fair and white. There was a beautiful pose about the neck and head which would have enraptured an artist.

As we peeped over the rags at the head, and then stepped round to the side to speak to it, the little one's face beamed forth with such a smile that it made us feel the tiny heart was but waiting for love as the flower buds wait for the sun —ready to burst forth at the first ray. The mother was at work, and the little one had to sit there 'on the bed during her absence. Ah ! many a long, dreary hour in the darkness and squalor had this little one to wait.

No sheets or blankets were upon the bed, only a common ticking covering and a few dirty rags for clothing. Some clothes hung drying on a line extended from two of the bed-posts, but the washing they had received seemed to have done very little to improve them. There were five more beds of the same description, with the ragged garments of the divers families ornamenting the strings and posts around them.

There was some water boiling on the stove, and there was a bench for us to sit upon as we talked to the occupants of the room. They knew the "Salvation Sisters," and were full of inquiries as to those who had been to visit them. Simply and earnestly, with first one and then another and then altogether, my companion pleaded. One face especially struck us as an intelligent, fine face. It was that of a man who had certainly seen far, far better days, but who, through the

strong chains of drink, had been dragged down until this
miserable, homeless place had become his only shelter. He
told us how he had recently attended our meetings on Four-
teenth Street, and he heard with interest of the opening of a
hall close by to which he said he would most certainly come
on Sunday. As we sang again we heard his voice chiming
in. When I prayed, the occupants of the room knelt down,

AFRAID OF ITS MOTHER.

and I could hear this man sobbing bitterly from the shadowy
corner where he knelt.

Heartsick, we turned into the landing, followed by the
" God bless you's! " of those who had just composed our little
audience.

Here a young woman came to open her sad heart to us, and
she told us how she would have to go to work for herself

directly she was well enough, for her husband was getting
worse and worse, and was drunk now all the time.

PRAYER-MEETING UNDER DIFFICULTIES.

Then down we passed another flight, and knocked at the
door of the lodging-room on the ground floor. On entering, we
found ourselves surrounded by strangers, for there had been
moving of families since my companion last visited there.
One man, however, remembered her, and welcomed us.
There were six double beds in this room also. It was very
much like the room above, only more wretched if anything.
The floor was as dirty, the windows as dark and the beds as
filthy with their trimmings of old rags. Ragged coats, sometimes crowned by battered-in, mould-covered hats, hung
upon the bedposts.

Here we had another prayer-meeting, and talked and sang
with the people, but were interrupted by a man who lay on a
bed, with his wife sitting at the foot drinking. Both of them
were drunk and resented our presence, while his wife began
working herself up into a very violent rage. However, we
were surprised to hear him chiming in as we sang, though they,
both of them, bounced out of the room when we prayed.
They returned afterward as we were saying good-bye, and we
took the opportunity to speak to them about their souls.

The man became interested, but his wife's rage knew no
bounds, and she informed us in very strong terms that he
was quite as good as we were, while in the next breath she
declared that priests, doctors, missionaries and ministers had
tried their level best to make him better and could not suc-
ceed—and it was pretty sure we should fail if they did. This
called forth answering abuse from him, and he demanded, in
very authoritative language, that she should immediately

"shut up and don't insult the ladies with your saucy tongue."
He, moreover, told her that she needed converting, and that
if she did not stop he would "throw her out of the window."
Then she dared him to do it, and so the quarrel went on.

We took our leave, followed by an assurance from the
woman that she wished us no harm, had never done anybody
any harm, and that she and her husband were a great deal
better than we were, which declaration seemed very much to
soothe her wounded feelings.

Then we passed out of the smoke, out of the foul, impure
air, into the chill and darkness of the night. Oh! how fresh
and fragrant seemed the breeze to us, though to uptown
dwellers it might have seemed fetid and fraught with every
imaginable bad odor. Very bright and clean looked our little
slum home as we entered. How dazingly white the fresh
scrubbed boards appeared after the dirty vermin-ridden
houses from which we had just come, and the eight white
plates round the table shone brilliantly.

Glad, indeed, were the little band of Slum workers for the
hot coffee and bread and butter, and as I looked round at the
faces of these girls—who so gladly and willingly give up the
comfort of ordinary life and live down in this darkness,
dressed in poor clothes, toiling and working, without money,
without praise and without thanks—I did not wonder that
they shed light into many a dark home, and brought comfort
into many a breaking heart.

Their faces were so bright and their voices so cheery that
you would have thought sunbeams instead of lamplight were
playing on their features. Truly they lived in the sunshine
of the smile of Him whom they love and serve, and it is this
brightness which they carry with them into the sin-stricken,
wretched homes which they visit,

JENNIE'S STORY.

As we knelt and prayed together, our hearts were stronger for what the night would bring. A few minutes we spent there, and then, allotting the different portions of the neighborhood to the girls, we prepared to go out again. But we paused for a moment as one of the girls came down from the nursery.

The last baby had just been taken away by its young eighteen-year-old mother. It was "Jennie's baby" that I had seen snugly wrapped up in the hammock ; and now she had come, after a hard day's work, to fetch him away.

All her week's earnings were contained in an envelope she held in her hand. Since Monday morning she had worked hard, and for all this toil had received $2 honestly hers. As she asked for change and opened the envelope that she might pay the daily five cents for her baby's keep to her horror she found that the $2 was missing. She had dropped it in the street, and she hastened away to retrace her steps through the darkness, while we all waited distressed and anxious. Gladly would we have given her the money, but we cannot give money, for instead of teaching self-help it would pauperize ; and when once given more is always expected. To our joy, however, she came back a few minutes later to say that she had picked it up upon the steps of a store but half a block away. Then, cheery and happy, she wrapped her baby round, and together they went out into the frost and darkness.

A sad story is hers ! Twelve months ago she visited the Slum quarters for the first time, despairing and sick at heart. She was only seventeen then, and she had a five-month-old baby in her arms—no home, no friends ; no one with whom to leave the little one, and hence no chance of getting work,

It meant to her either shame or starvation. For weeks past she had slept with her babe in entryways and washed him daily under the hydrants. How thankful she was when he was taken into the nursery and she could gain an honest living ! But the baby was always ailing and died at last, and the little one which now takes its place has better fare, for he is a daily occupant of the nursery, and his mother is supporting them both by honest work.

VISITING THE DIVES.

Out into the night again went the little band, two and two, scattered for night work with the teeming crowds that turned midnight to noonday. Saloon and dive visiting was the order of the night, and though it was not yet very late we found all the men and women drunk in the first saloon we entered. Hardly able to stand, they were leaning about on tables and against the wall, quarreling and drinking, and inhaling the fumes of the worst tobacco I have ever smelled.

One man became angry, saying that he did not need us, and that he was a Catholic. But then some native honesty lurking in his befogged brain made him add, " I know I ought to be a good Catholic, and am a bad one, more's the pity." Before we parted he was the most respectful and most interested member of our little audience. We were asked in rather a definite manner to "quit," and so we passed out of the glare and smoke into the night.

At the next door we heard the sound of music. A violin, piano and flute were rattling off, loudly and shrilly, the quickest of dance music. We pushed open the screen doors and found ourselves in a large room where there were six or seven young girls in brilliant short dresses drinking, dancing and laughing with a low, dissolute crowd of men. Oh, how difficult it is to deal with those whose hearts are aching, but

RETIRING IN A LODGING HOUSE.

who toss their heads and laugh, and walk away to dance the dance of death, or to toss off spirits as if they were drinking water! We talked with each one of them, and then passed out again to another.

Both sides of the street—to the right and to the left, in front of us and behind—are crowded, and we hear the sounds of music and laughter and the shrill wrangling of those already drunk. I could go on describing at length the work which every week is done patiently and carefully in these haunts of vice and sin, but I must pass on.

BY THE WAYSIDE.

Perhaps the most interesting work of that evening was the quiet talks we had with the men lounging on the sidewalks. Every now and then we would be interrupted by the drunken companion of one to whom we were speaking, or a woman (without womanhood) would appear on the threshold of one of those places and try to persuade or taunt our listener into leaving us and joining the crowd within.

We talked to a pale-faced boy dressed in threadbare clothing, whose face was so pallid and ghastly that it looked as if disease was already the forerunner of near approaching death. He was only fourteen! He lived in a saloon, and in his young life had already seen more of vice and sin than a volume could unfold.

"Never mind, if smoking and drinking may seem to you to make you more manly, you know it really makes—" But before she could finish the sentence he chimed in with—

"I know it makes fools of men. It would make a fool of me."

And the bitterness in his voice showed us plainly that he realized the end of the broad path down which those many dancing feet were so swiftly treading,

My companion was speaking to a man a few steps away, when I began a conversation with a bright-eyed, good-natured sailor lad, and found that he was a backslider. Fully realizing the wretchedness and misery that those haunts harbored behind their light and music, he still said that after weeks of weary work at sea they were a sailor's only welcome to shore again.

I could see, as he tried to laugh off what I was saying to him, that he felt more than he cared to say. "It's all right —it's all right! But it's no good talking to me," he said ; and then I asked him—looking into eyes that were frank and honest despite the apparent indifference :—"Do you not be; lieve that this religion we talk about is real? Do you think we are in earnest or not?" "In earnest! Of course you are ! We all know that. Why you go into dens and places where others cannot and dare not enter, for it would be as much as their lives are worth. But we know you." I inwardly said, "Thank God !" as these words showed me that The Salvation Army is gaining the confidence of the class for whom they mostly work. With a warm nand-grip we parted, and I saw him wistfully looking after us as we walked on.

Many others were talked to—hopeless ones, starving ones, staggering drunkards—and then back again we went to hear from the other Slum saviours of their visits in fifteen saloons.

CHAPTER IX.

PATROLLING THE STREETS.

A FEW more minutes together and we turn out again to pass the midnight hours on the streets.

It is very dark and cold now. Cats prowl about, growling in the ash barrels, running out from unsuspected nooks and corners, fighting under the empty wagons that line the streets, stealing down cellar stairs and darting about here, there and everywhere. These vagrant cats seem to be the only well-fed inhabitants of the slums, and it is a good thing perhaps that they are there to help to clear the refuse from the streets.

On, down street after street, until we walked into the glare of the Bowery. Men and women pass us in scores, and hundreds throng the streets as midnight approaches. Young girls, laughing loud and long, old men tottering along with the tide of passers-by, or leaning against some post or pillar ; young men, some in tatters, with pinched and hungry features, some with flashy dress and with the stamp of vice upon their faces.

We were crossing the street when I became aware of a band of drunken men just behind us. I could hear their talk. and when we gained the other side and hurried on I thought they were still following.

Suddenly my arm was tightly gripped ! I drew it away and turned to confront the man who had taken it, when I heard the words :—

"Don't you know me?" and a tall figure leaned over me. The face was smeared with dirt, the clothes were ragged, the hat was battered, but in spite of that I knew him—it was my *husband!*

I had to struggle hard to keep an exclamation of joy and a smile of glad recognition from lighting my face, but we were the observed of all observers, with the light shining brightly on my Army badge, and I knew only too well that any affectionate look of recognition bestowed upon this (supposed) street tough would be misunderstood. So, with a short, earnest word or two and with a parting "God bless you!" I handed him a tract and we plunged again into the throng.

It was Sunday morning now. Some saloons were still open and crowded ; the front doors of others had been closed, but through the cracks of the blinds and shutters we could still see crowds within, and the side doors, we found, had been opened.

SUNDAY MORNING SIDE DOORS.

The side entrances to the saloons seemed every whit as bad as the front, and quite as many people seemed to go into them. Pool rooms were thronged, and billiard rooms also, while up and down the streets the stream of passers still flowed on, and every hour appeared more ghastly by the glare of the electric light.

The walk of many was growing more and more unsteady, and some of the homeless, shivering unemployed who could not pay for a night's lodging, had slunk back into the doorways and were bracing themselves up against the sides. The degradation and villainy written plainly upon some faces we met was enough to make any heart shudder ; and it was brought into greater prominence by the refined, and, in some instances, beautiful faces of the hapless girls who were their companions.

Then in the early morning hours, as we retraced our steps again into the back streets, staggering figures were seen on all sides. Here was a policeman rousing and waking a drunken man, who lay stupefied and sleeping in an entry, but who had to get up and stagger away into the darkness, only to fall a little further on and be roused and driven forward by another policeman, and further on by yet another and another.

DEFERENCE TO SALVATION GIRLS.

But even these staggering drunkards tried to step out of our way and let us pass when they saw The Army badge and recognized us as Salvationists. A little ragged, tattered boy was running swiftly past us, and when he saw who we were raised his tattered little cap with a wave of recognition and a smile. And I thanked God from the depth of my heart that the patient toil of these last months had done its work, and had found a place for these brave girls in the hearts of those for whom they live and work and sacrifice.

Away above us we could see glimmering like stars in the darkness the brilliant lights of the Brooklyn Bridge; cold and clear and mocking they looked as they shone out of the darkness, and their glimmer was reflected in the muddy pools at our feet. Over that bridge passed daily hundreds and thousands from home to office and office to home, knowing nothing of the dying, starving, sin-blighted multitudes in the hot-bed of wretchedness beneath. Mocking lights of Brooklyn Bridge! You cannot lighten this darkness! But above, looking down with pitying love and mercy, we felt there was One whose eyes can pierce not only the darkness of the gathering clouds but also the darkness of vice and sin—One who can help us seek and save these wandering lost ones.

Still the strains of music came from behind the closed doors of the saloons, though the streets were desolate, save for some forlorn figures, reeling now against a lamp-post, now against the shutters of some store, and the upright form of the police officer hovering in their wake and watching every suspicious figure that glided in and out and round about the dark shadows.

A sheltering oasis, our tiny room in the back tenement house, seemed to us that night, and, weary and footsore as we were, the little trundle bed was wonderfully welcome. And it seemed soft to us when we thought of the many who were sleeping in those empty carts or tramping the streets all night, or lying upon filthy rags in the fetid air of the lodging-house we had visited.

I cannot tell how it was that I managed to fall asleep at all, for I felt as though sleep was the last thing possible. But somehow or other my eyes closed, and then I found myself in a thrilling and exciting situation, in the midst of a crowd of men in a pool-room or a cellar, and I was trying to drive out some boys who were there, and talking to the drunken wretch who, I felt, had entrapped them to the ruin of their souls.

From these scenes I was aroused. The room was light, and dreams and shadows fled away as I heard a clear, happy voice singing down below, " Hallelujah ! Hallelujah ! I love Thee, my Saviour, I trust, Lord, in Thee." And then, looking up, I could see from my window some smoky chimneys and the tower of Brooklyn Bridge, and I realized that the night with its horrors was over.

WRECKAGE OF THE NIGHT TIDE.

But daylight only ushered in a day with more heart-breaking scenes, more weariness and sadness, as we saw the wreckage cast up by the stream of dissipation of the night before. A very lively fight was going on in the yard below between four wretched-looking cats, and shortly afterward a sound of quarreling (this time in the human family) reminded us that the "still calm of Sabbath" is a thing unknown in slumdom.

I thought as we all knelt together in prayer around the breakfast table and I listened to the clear ringing voices and comforting words sung, how many of the despairing neighbors must listen and be cheered by sounds so different to those that clashed upon our ears, making the day miserable and the stillness of night bristle with horror. Cries of murder, the thud of falling blows, and the shrieks of women are familiar sounds! Their ears are accustomed to ribald, obscene songs and peals of laughter, both hollow and false, showing bitterness and woe unspoken. Like a fresh breeze to becalmed sailors or the scent of violets to the fever-stricken patient must seem the happy, cheery voices and the pure, hope-breathing words wafted from the little Slum home in the tenement house.

> Oh for trust that brings the triumph,
> When defeat seems strangely near!
> Oh for faith that changes fighting
> Into victory's ringing cheer!
> Faith triumphant!
> Knowing not defeat or fear.

We sang over and over again, and it was not mere empty sentiment.

The light of true faith shone on each face, and the determination to fight and suffer until each effort was crowned with victory rang in the earnest voices. Ah! no one but God knows how much faith and trust and courage is needed by these Slum officers, who become one with the outcast poor in

home and dress and work, that they may tread in the steps
of Christ and for His dear sake win back those lost sheep.

CHAPTER X

BRAVERY OF THE ARMY GIRLS.

H IDDEN haunts of darkest vice, saloons, dives, lodging houses and dens of ill repute are alike visited. They fearlessly enter everywhere into the shadows, with no man or detective or escort to protect them, knowing that around them are thrown the everlasting arms of Him who can best guard them.

Patiently, lovingly and bravely they are working on, day and night! Unknown are they by the outer world, without honor, without recognition and often without the thanks of those whom they strive to help. But God sees, and each act done unto Him is chronicled.

Again we wrapped our shawls about us and paired off for the day's visiting. But just before leaving the house we were startled by the sound of high words and angry voices. One of the girls went out to see what was the matter, and found that it was "another row" between some neighbors, of whom the girl spoke by name ; and just then the man was heard threatening loudly to throw his wife over the stairs.

The great feature of Sunday visiting is invariably the large number of people found drunk in their own homes. The revels of the previous night seem to tell all round on men and women alike.

Our first visit was in a cellar. Down the dirty sawdust-strewn steps we stumbled into a low, damp place where kindling wood lay about in piles, and stacks of lumber still waiting to be chopped forced us to carefully pick our way. A lamp was nailed upon a beam and gave a little light.

No stranger looking in would have supposed that human beings lived there!   But my companion went straight up to the little partitioned off corner, which looked like a small shed in which a goat could be kept, and through the chinks and holes in the boards we could see a light from within, for no daylight penetrated to the spot.

MISERABLE OLD AGE.

LIVING IN A CELLAR CUPBOARD.

A voice from within answered the knock, and we opened

the door. There was not room for us both to enter, so I stood in the doorway and my companion went just inside.

So small was the place that it could not be called anything but a cupboard. This was rented as a " furnished room," and the rent was $6. The furniture consisted of a stove, in which fortunately there was a fire, a table and two chairs. My companion told me that the last time the poor old couple were visited there was not a bit of warmth to counteract the damp chill of the cellar.

At the table sat an old man, certainly past sixty, and his aged wife. Behind some old rags and clothes hanging from the side just behind the man was a bed, if it could be called such.

After some talk we sang and prayed, and I could hardly find room to kneel down.

There was no ventilation, no daylight and no comfort, and as we picked our way out again through the wood cellar I heard how they had first been found by our girls. One of them had stopped to talk to the old woman, who had been sitting despondently upon the steps, and following her into her room had found the poor shed she called home. Still the fact of being to themselves must make life in this cellar preferable to that in the lodging house. As we climbed the steps again I caught my feet in my ragged dress, and picked myself up again to find a tear half a yard long embellishing the front of it.

A few steps further and we dived down a narrow alley-way and reached a rear tenement house. In this house some thirty families live, crowded into small rooms—men, women and children—most of them squalid, drunken and quarrel-some in the extreme.

BABY JIM.

It was in one of the topmost rooms that we had found a poor baby boy (some time since), whose grandfather assured us "only lived out of spite," and whose wasted little body and one ragged garment spoke louder than words of neglect and misery.

That house will always make me think of Baby Jim and the long, weary hours he must have spent sobbing ; for his mother used to go out and lock him up all alone, and he had lain on the bare boards until his little back was covered with sores.

One day the slum officers called and found the door locked, but while she was knocking at it the mother returned and opened it. They entered, and found the poor baby sitting beneath the table, his face swollen with tears and his little body filthy. As his mother stooped to drag him up, with a cry he shrank from her.

" Where is Baby Jim now ? " I asked.

"His mother is dead," answered my companion. Only eighteen, and yet she had led such a dissolute life that, like many others of these girls, she had died very suddenly, almost as you might blow out the flame of a candle.

And Baby Jim has been taken away and has not been found again. Let us hope that some white-winged angel has carried him away from the wretchedness and squalor to the peace and love which he never knew on earth.

The stairs are of stone, but they are narrow and dirty, and the air is bad. The smells are sickening.

A very warm welcome awaited us in the first room we entered, and it was a bright, honest face that lighted up with smiles at our visit. Clear, blue, Irish eyes and wavy black hair had the mother, while the girl and boy, whose

morning toilet was being performed, were little copies of her.
The young husband sat on the couch, and the old mother at
the table. Another girl who was staying with them made up
the rest of the family, all of whom lived in those two small
rooms.

A change had crept into this home. There was food to
eat, and the children had new clothes, for the mother had
stopped drinking. When first found by our workers the
woman was hopelessly enchained by that soul and body
blighting enemy. In a squalid, filthy room of a house of bad
repute she was drinking with two men, in shameless, bold
attire.

No food had been in the house that day, and one hungry
child gnawed at a raw onion while they sat in a corner
watching their mother. As the Slum girls entered and began
to talk with her the men slunk out ; and a wave of bitter
remorse, swept over the poor girl as she listened to their
words. She arose and paced the room, tearing her raven
black tresses.

"Oh, God help me! God forgive me! I know—I know I
am lost! It is all the drink—the drink! Seventy-five cents
gone in drink already this morning, and not a bit of food in
the house for my children! My darlings! Only twenty-four
—only twenty-four—and I'm a drunkard—a drunkard!"

Pausing before her children, with voice broken and
pathetic in the extreme, she cried :—

"Oh, my children! My poor children! You have no
mother! She is a drunkard—a drunkard!" And the black
hair was torn again.

Her husband was in jail at that time, still she could make
good money at her work. But, alas! it all went in drink.

CHAPTER XI.

GLIMPSES OF SUNLIGHT.

L OVING, patient, pleading, many visits and faith-wrought prayers won this heart (really very honest and with many redeeming features), and a strong bond of sympathy sprang up between her and her new friends.

She moved into more respectable quarters, and then her husband returned. He, too, drank, and drinks still, but she has now got a little home, keeps herself looking clean and bright, and her earnings are rightly spent.

Joyfully she showed the new dress she had bought for her bright little girl, and then told us how she had been getting on. She had been tempted often, and had sometimes given way again to drink.

"But your words always, always come back to me," she said, turning to my companion, "and they have all come true every time!" Now she "had done with the drink," she said, "done with it forever." So with the prayer that He who alone could give her the power to live out this resolution and keep her from falling might be near her, we turned away, thankful for this little gleam of sunlight in the sad visits of the day.

From behind each door as we climbed the winding stairs came sounds of quarreling, drunkenness and sin. In describing one I can pretty nearly describe all. We knocked at a door from behind which issued loud and coarse words.

"Come in !" shrieked a chorus of women's voices. It was a small and wretched room, with another one, cramped and dark as a cupboard, opening out of it. Its occupants were three women, two men and a babe. One woman was inclined to resent our entrance, but after a few sharp words disappeared into the back room with the sickly baby. The other two were civil, even pleased to see us.

The two men were in a besotted state—we might say literally soaked with drink. Of course, there was no carpet on the floor; dirt and disorder reigned, and the fumes of drink and stale tobacco made the air thick and poisonous.

While I was talking to the girl-mother about her baby and its future and the effect of her present life and surroundings upon him, I could hear my companion talking earnestly to the men, and their incoherent and sometimes uncivil answers. When these every now and then reached beyond the limit of slum etiquette, the two women shouted in chorus :—

"Ah ! Patsey, now can't yer hold yer saucy tongue ! You're beastly drunk, anyway ! Shut up, and let us hear the ladies. It's kind of them to call to see us !"

And Patsey would roll back against the wall for a few moments, pause, and try to collect his scattered senses before again joining in the conversation.

TAKEN BY THE NURSERY PLAN.

The women were really interested, and said :—

"Please don't yer take no notice of the men. They're awful rough, and don't know how to treat yer. But yer see how it is, they're full—and more's the pity !" This family were newcomers to the house, but had heard of us from neighbors.

"And is it true yer have a nursery fur babies?" they asked.

There was a lull in the storm. Patsey rolled about undecidedly, perhaps wondering which of us to accost, and fearing another wifely reproof, and that which might accompany and emphasize it.

" Yes," we answered, " we have a nursery, and sometimes take as many as sixteen babies."

" Well, I never ! And can one fetch the baby away again at night after work hours ? "

" Yes."

" And is there any one there to look after 'em and see they're all right ? " continued the young mother, her face all interest.

" Yes, indeed," we answered.　" Two girls to care for them, and nice little beds, and toys, and swings, and milk ; and they all look so clean and happy."

A BEAUTY AMONG THE FILTH.

"Well, well," chimed in the older woman, "and how much is there to pay?"

"Five cents a day," we answered.

"Five cents a day—only five cents! Well, did you ever! Only five cents! That is fine." The women were filled with wonder, and then confided to us that the little mother was going to work on her own account, if only she had some one to "do right by the baby" in her absence, and the possibility of taking him home at night.

Oh, how these mothers still cling to their babies, and I do not wonder! They want something to love, something that will love them in return, something to cling to and live for, or—well, life would be too hard, too cold and too cruel to endure, and the cold, lapping waters of the East River would be welcome kisses, wooing to the oft-thought-of deliverance—death!

But to return to my story. Our conversation was brought to an end by the men who appeared deaf to the entreaties to "shut up" and be "ashamed of yerselves," etc. So we took leave, and the women whispered:—

"Thank you kindly. Come again to see us when the men ain't here, and don't you mind them—don't be upset by them, they be beastly drunk!"

We smilingly assured them that our feelings were not hurt, and our reception should not make us hesitate in calling again.

CHAPTER XII.

FOR HIS DEAR SAKE.

IN the next room our welcome was even warmer. Two women were violently drunk, while the men were staggering and stupid. The tables were turned here, however, and the caustic, abusive language of one of the women was roundly denounced by the man, who asked her if she couldn't " trate the ladies dacent."

What a hubbub—what language—and, oh ! what faces ! No woman's face could be imagined much more marred, degraded and bloated. A regular virago ; bare arms raised threateningly, hair a dirty, tangled mop, features swelled, bloated flesh hanging in baggy folds, and—such a tongue !

" No, I don't want yer—go away—I have my praste ! I'm a good Catholic, and I know lots better than you all about religion—get out !"

Here she was stopped by one of the men and had an aside with the other woman, who was evidently coaching her for the second attack. Meanwhile the man took down a crucifix and showed it to us.

" That's my religion, ladies ! and this is the only one in the whole house ! You won't find another one in any room here ! There, ladies !"

We assured him that the dear crucified Lord was our God, and that it was in memory of that cross that we tried to do all we could in a neighborly way for those around us.

" Say ! say !" shouted the woman, " can you bless yerself in Latin ? Can you ? Listen ?" and in the loudest soprano

she proceeded to do so, while the others watched to see the
effect of this learning upon us. I glanced around the room.
It was dirty and in a state of chaos. In the inner room
kindling wood and filthy bedding were mixed in a ruined pile.
But my thoughts were speedily brought back.

"Now I tell yer I don't want yer! I've got my praste!"
Here we interrupted.

"Yes, we don't say anything about your priest or your religion, except that you should do as your priest tells you. He
does not tell you to get drunk and sin and live like this. You
are not a good Catholic. That's the trouble. We want to
help people to be good and serve God; and we don't say
that it is the name that is wrong, but the *life*."

"And then with a few parting words of assurance that
we did not come there to preach at or to anger them, but
only to cheer or help them and to say a kind word, we
parted.

CHRISTIANITY, LIFE NOT CREED.

Down the dirty staircase we tramped—heartsick and
tired—reflecting with sorrow on the fact that in slumdom, as
in society, people haggle over the name, the creed, the
belief, and neglect the essence of religion—the *life*.

Catholics, Protestants, infidels, alike we visit in these
sinful, wretched haunts, and to all our message is the same.
It is goodness, pureness, that alone can make life happy,
prosperous and peaceful here—and the future Heaven ours.
And then we show them how the death and love of Christ
can make it possible for us to live such a life.

By patient, loving work—washing of dirty children, nurs-
ing of sick ones, comforting of those in sorrow—the slum
workers give them a practical object lesson in what religion
really is. We had visited newcomers to the district that day

who did not know us, hence our warm reception—for in
hundreds of poor homes the girls are welcomed as "angels of
light." Aye, and even sent for at all hours when there
is trouble or sickness.

Again we found ourselves in the street, and the fresh air
was indeed welcome.   I felt sick and so tired that my steps
were unsteady, and I had to take my companion's arm and
brace up for fear of appearing as staggering as our neighbors
are wont to be on Sundays.

On reaching our slum quarters we found a man sitting at
the table much enjoying a cup of warm coffee and some
bread and butter. He was very poor, and his face bore
marks of great suffering, but he was cheery and hopeful.

SAVED, ALTHOUGH A TRAMP.

"No, he has not yet got work, only odd jobs once in a
while."

There were "an awful lot of men hanging around out of
work" and times were hard, but he hoped better days
would dawn for him in the coming week.

His face brightened as he spoke, and I learned after
he had gone, that through the words of our officers he had
given his heart to God, and his life, so far as sin and
drink were concerned, had shown a decided change ; though,
alas ! he is still in the great army of "out-of-works." He
came to New York some months ago as a stowaway on ship-
board after a long illness in the hospital of a far away
foreign port. He reached here homeless, friendless and
moneyless, and for weeks his only shelter for the night was
a pile of lumber behind which he crept. He heard of our
workers and came to them almost in despair, but now the
despair is gone, though the poverty still faces him.

As I laid aside my hat and leaned back for a minute's

rest before our mid-day meal, I called my companion to me and said :

" Now tell me about that poor baby girl whose frightful story I heard the other day. Did she live after the brutal treatment she received?"

The tears came into her eyes as she answered,

" No! poor little thing. She died ! The whole story is a pitiful one ! "

And then I heard the following tale of poverty and crime :—

The family lived in a little back room behind a small tinker store. When first visited the mother—only about twenty-four years of age—was found in this little room with two children, one about three years and the other a few months old. Both of the children were naked and she had not a garment to put on them. They were very poor, and, alas! young as she was, she already was a hopeless drink victim. A few more visits and the store was found vacant ; but we followed them up and found that the father had had to move from the store into a cellar and that the mother and children were living in one of the worst lodging houses of the district.

The father was a respectable young man, steady and honest, and tried to do all he could for the wife and children whom he really loved. But what could he do? She was like a millstone around his neck, and the vile companionship of the lodging house made her sink lower rapidly.

One night he called at our quarters in despair. Tears were coursing down his face, and he said :—

" I can't tell what to do for my wife ! She is nearly mad ! Can I bring her to you ? "

On receiving an answer in the affirmative, he hurried out into the night and soon returned with the woman, Wildly she paced up and down the room groaning in some unutterable agony, and every now and then shrieking and talking incoherently. What was it? Our girls looked at her in wonder.

For a minute or two she would seem calm, and looking up into the faces around her she would say :—

"Oh, you're so good—so good, and I'm so bad—so bad. Don't despise me. Don't give me up because I'm so bad. Oh, help me—help me! For God's sake help me!"

And then she would start wildly up and shriek again.

Suddenly it dawned upon our girls that the first symptoms of *delirium tremens* were manifested thus. Telling her husband to get her home and to bed as soon as he could they went out with him to see her safely home, and to get the two children, whom they had promised to keep while she was at the hospital. After she came out again she came for the children. They were kept in the nursery by day and she came and fetched them at night.

"DRUNK AGAIN."

Often she would sit with despair written upon her haggard face, sobbing,

"Oh, my Gracie, my Mamie! My Gracie, my Mamie! My poor, poor children!"

And yet, with all her desire to be good, the fiend seemed to have a firm grip upon this poor victim. Again, late one night, she came to the girls in the throes of delirium. They could not turn her out, for she pitifully clung to them and pleaded with them to keep her. So they locked her into one of their little rooms, taking from her anything with which she could commit suicide, and there through the dread night they watched and cared for her.

HOPE EVEN FOR SUCH AS THIS AND THOUSANDS MORE.

Her youngest child is in the sunny land where no sorrows dwell. The husband in despair has given up the hope of ever reclaiming his poor, drink-ridden young wife and has left her. Still many, many such despairing ones are being reclaimed and their lives brightened by a power even stronger than the infernal chains that bind them.

Other stories, other scenes and sights rise up before me, but I can write no more. I have come back into the rush and whirl of the busy life of the city; but still down in the darkness are working ten true, brave, loving girls day and night facing scenes such as I have described, and sometimes even far more terrible ones than these. It is difficult for me to shake off the experience.

It is now over, and I am trying to write sounds and sights which still surge to and fro in my memory. But as I look back over the pages I have written, I feel it is hopeless to reproduce that which must be seen and felt and heard to be understood.

No wonder our hearts ache! No wonder we long to do more, far more, in the future than we have ever done in the past to alleviate this suffering, this raging stream of vice, and to raise these fallen ones, to speak hope to the hopeless, and bring sunshine into the darkness and horror of New York's hell.

Maud B Booth

FINIS.

THE SALVATION ARMY FIELD STATE, DECEMBER, 1890.

(In several instances one name includes several countries or colonies.)

Country.	Headquarters	Corps or Societies.	Officers
BRITISH ISLES.	101 Queen Victoria Street, London, E.C. Home Offices, 179 Queen Victoria Street.	1,304	4,624
UNITED STATES OF AMERICA.	111 Reade Street, New York	445	1,150
FRANCE AND SWITZERLAND.	Rue Auber, 3, Paris	109	389
BELGIUM.	32 Boulevard Badouin, Brussels.	4	26
HOLLAND.	Rapenburg, 44, Amsterdam.	42	155
GERMANY.	Friederichstrasse, 214, Berlin.	22	75
DENMARK.	Helgesensgade, 11, 13 and 15, Copenhagen	36	103
SWEDEN.	Ostermalmsgaten, 33 and 35, Stockholm...	108	373
NORWAY.	Pilestradet, 22, Christiania.	47	142
CANADA AND NEWFOUNDLAND.	Salvation Temple, Toronto.	313	1,056
ARGENTINE REPUBLIC.	422 Cassilla de Corres, Buenos Ayres...	4	2
SOUTH AFRICA.	Kimberley.	54	165
ST. HELENA.	James Town.	1	2
INDIA AND CEYLON.	Esplanade, Bombay	100	425
AUSTRALIA.	185 Little Collins Street, Melbourne.	281	991
NEW ZEALAND.	48 Manchester Street, Christchurch.	66	193
FINLAND.	Michaelsgaten, 27, Helsingfors.	5	21
Total.		3,001	9,896
" for 1889.		2,746	8,634
Increase.		255	1,262

THE SALVATION ARMY'S STANDING IN THE UNITED STATES.

JANUARY, 1891.

Number of Corps and Outposts...   445
Number of Officers.............................   1,150
Combined Weekly Circulation of three *War Crys*—
    New York and San Francisco, and Swedish
    War Cry (New York).....................   53,000
Number of States occupied................   35
Number of Hours spent by Officers in Visitation
    during 1890...................................   389,000
Number of Families Visited by Officers during 1890   547,000
Number of Persons Professing Conversion between
    December 1, 1889, and December 1, 1890.......   23,562
Number of Open-air Services during 1890..........   46,800
Number of Persons estimated as Attending our
    Open-air Meetings, 1890..................   4,000,000
Number of Persons Attending our Meetings during
    October, 1890...............................   1,070,000
Number of Persons Attending Meetings during
    the Year....   12,000,000
Rescue Homes.................................   2
Slum Posts....................................   2
Training Garrisons at New York, Brooklyn, Boston
    (2), Detroit, Grand Rapids, Englewood, Ill.,
    Des Moines, Omaha, Oakland, Cal., and San
    Francisco.................................   10

NOTICE !

SYMPATHY MATERIALIZED.

HOW ALMOST ANYBODY MAY AID THE SALVATION ARMY WORK.

No one who has not been engaged in this work can understand how much help is needed to carry it on successfully year after year. We realize that many who cannot possibly give their lives up to seek and personally administer comfort to the poor, long to do something, and yet possibly they also find themselves financially unable to assist much those who are doing the work. This may lead them to feel that their interest will have to end in mere sympathy ; but this need not be.

Our workers are all the time in need of clothing for women and children. Babies with absolutely nothing to cover them, or else with clothing so filthy that it has to be burned before we can take them in, are met with daily, and the cast-off garments of more fortunate little ones would be indeed a blessing to them. If any of the readers of the *Herald* would like to send parcels of—to them useless—clothes, address to 111 Reade street, New York City. We can promise to use them to the best advantage in bringing comfort where it is most needed.

May we also add that never in the history of our movement in this country could we make a better use of money for the practical advancement of work among the poor than at the present time. Those who cannot go themselves into the darkness of New York's hell to rescue its victims, who cannot visit the saloons or stem the tide of godless debauchery that is devastating our country, can, by proxy, reach forth the hand of sympathy by giving us the means to do it. Let us remind those who are interested in " New York's inferno " of the words, " Inasmuch as ye have done it unto one of the least of these, my brethren, ye have done it unto Me."

Believe us, yours truly in the holy war,

BALLINGTON BOOTH.
MAUD B. BOOTH.

BENEATH TWO FLAGS:

THE AIM, METHODS OF WORK AND HISTORY OF

THE SALVATION ARMY.

BY MRS. BALLINGTON BOOTH.

Illustrated, 12mo., cloth, 288 pp. Price $1, post free.

This volume furnishes its readers with every needful particular concerning this growing organization of over 1,000,000 adherents, which, having spread out its branches throughout Great Britain, is making rapid progress also in the United States.

THE

WAR  CRY,

THE OFFICIAL GAZETTE OF THE SALVATION ARMY,

Consists of sixteen pages, sixty-four columns, with illustrations, and contains the latest intelligence of the progress of the Salvation Army work in ALL PARTS OF THE WORLD ;

Stories of Wonderful Conversions ; Original Salvation Songs ; Lives of Prominent Salvation Officers,

WITH PORTRAITS AND OTHER ILLUSTRATIONS.

EVERY SATURDAY.

Price 5c. ; Yearly Subscription, $2.00 postpaid.

WHAT IS AN AUXILIARY ?

There are many members of the community who view with sorrow and pity the misery and vice to be seen on every hand. Not a few of these are occupied themselves in evangelistic work, while others do not profess, or even possess religion of any kind.

Although such friends cannot be soldiers in The Army, they can help us with means and sympathy and influence in our efforts to deal with evil ; and this rather more than less perhaps because they do not, by joining the League, endorse, or even approve all the methods we employ.

We rely upon the Auxiliary League to assist us by means of prayer, sympathy, influence and money.

We also desire Auxiliaries to

Use their Personal Influence

on our behalf, by letting it be known that they are not against us, and by defending us from the effects of many misrepresentations of ourselves and our motives. They can help us by obtaining explanations of specific matters, by stating facts concerning our work to their friends, or by making communications to the local press calculated to remove false impressions.

Auxiliaries can help by gifts of money. In the United States the cost of the necessary oversight, though kept down as much as possible, is very great. Help must be given to officers who require rest on account of sickness ; while the Slum work and our Rescue operations, being only in their infancy as yet, are unable to sustain themselves.

The annual subscription to the League is **Five Dollars,** and this secures the *War Cry* or *All the World* and the *Deliverer*, at the option of the subscriber, mailed free for twelve months. A handsome leather badge is also sent to each member, the production of which will secure a hearty welcome to any gathering in any country, and a pin is also furnished, which can be worn on the dress, show it in that way. Like the badge, it will be recognized in any part of the world.

Captain EDITH MARSHALL, who has charge of the Auxiliary Department, will be happy to answer any inquiries, or supply any information that members of the League may desire at any time.

All remittances should be made out in favor of BALLINGTON BOOTH, 111 READE ST., NEW YORK CITY.

www.ingramcontent.com/pod-product-compliance
Lightning Source LLC
Chambersburg PA
CBHW032153010726
47493CB00008BA/2678